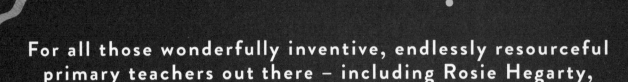

For all those wonderfully inventive, endlessly resourceful
primary teachers out there – including Rosie Hegarty,
who created the spark that became this book.

JC

To Elsa, Hannah, Amy, Cléophée, Arthur, Basile, Indy,
Louis, Léon and all the kool kids of the 21st century.
And to my devil 20th century baby sister, you are still
my favourite.

MC

CATERPILLAR BOOKS
An imprint of the LITTLE TIGER GROUP
1 Coda Studios, 189 Munster Road, London SW6 6AW
Imported into the EEA by Penguin Random House Ireland,
Morrison Chambers, 32 Nassau Street, Dublin D02 YH68
www.littletiger.co.uk • First published in Great Britain 2022
Text copyright © James Carter 2022
Illustrations copyright © Margaux Carpentier 2022
A CIP catalogue record for this book
is available from the British Library
All rights reserved • ISBN: 978-1-83891-393-9
Printed in China • CPB/1400/2035/1121
2 4 6 8 10 9 7 5 3 1

FSC
www.fsc.org
MIX
Paper from
responsible sources
FSC® C104723

The Forest Stewardship Council ® (FSC®) is an international,
non-governmental organisation dedicated to promoting responsible
management of the world's forests. FSC operates a system of forest
certification and product labelling that allows consumers to identify
wood and wood-based products from well-managed forests
and other controlled sources.

For more information about the FSC,
please visit their website at www.fsc.org

The story of inventions

Once upon a big idea

James Carter

Illustrated by Margaux Carpentier

With a whizz, fizz,
zip, zap,
tick, tock,
click, clack.

And a beep, bleep,
whoosh, whirr...

welcome to
our modern world!

Rockets, robots,
turbo engines,
wow, we've got some
great

inventions...

Telescopes
and clocks and trains –
all **big ideas**
from human

brains!

something **new.**

and

turn

it

into

is what

we

do

Take

something **old**

We work it, **shape** it,

chop and **change** it.

All the while we **recreate** it...

Rocks
and **stones**
were all around

in easy reach and
underground...

For making tools and walls and bricks,

with which

we'd build the pyramids.

Animals gave fur and hides.

Meat to eat and more besides.

Hardy clothes and sturdy shoes.

Wool to weave.

From bones, more tools.

Wood, we learnt, could bend, could float, build **homes** and **bridges**,

craft us **boats**.

The best **invention** of all time?

Perhaps the

wheel.

It changed our lives!

From **sand** came **glass**.

But what from **clay**? Pots and pipes, cups and plates.

With **fire**, we'd **cook**,

have **heat** and **light**.

illuminate

the darkest **night**.

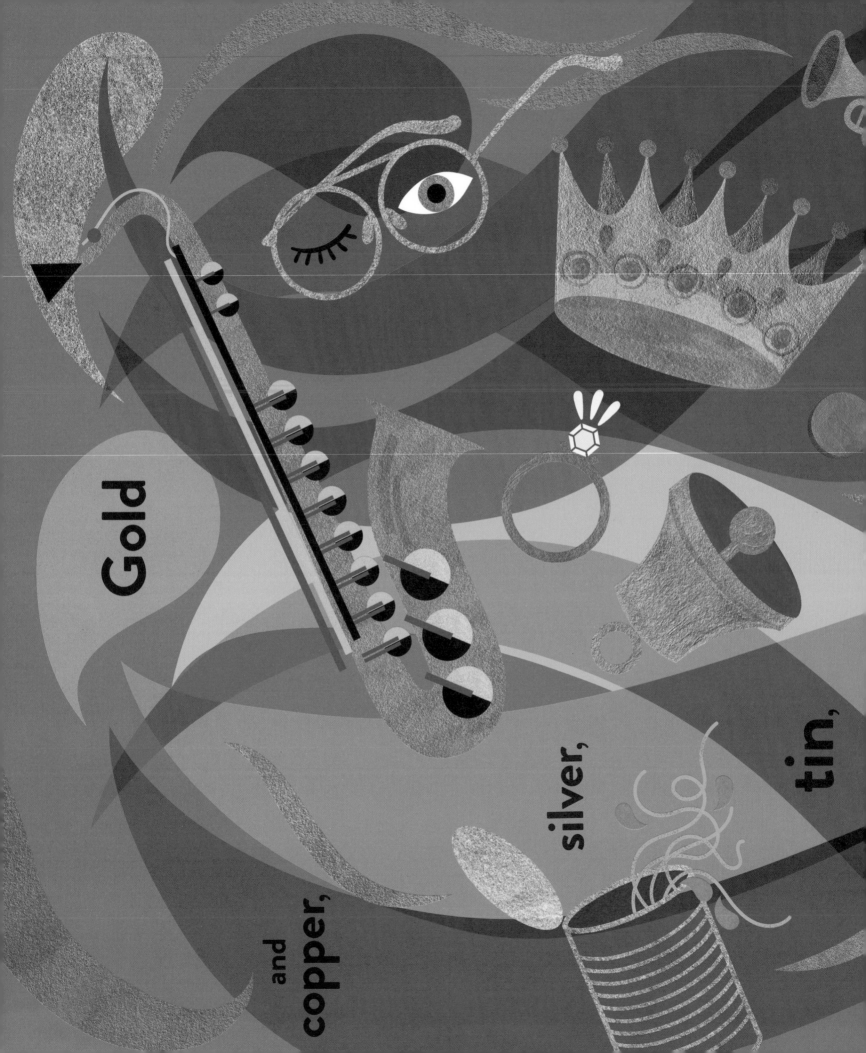

Gold

and
copper,

silver,

tin,

Materials
that we'd create
encouraged us
to **innovate**.

With **rubber** – tyres,
from **cotton** – clothes,
with **nylon** – nets
and **concrete** – roads.

Books would come
from **paper, ink;**
from **plastic** – bottles,
packaging.

Now many screens fill modern homes –
computers, TVs, mobile phones.

Machines are **useful,**

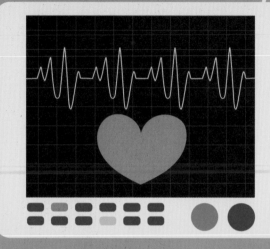

crucial, clever.

What's **your** best **invention** ever?

As we produce so much these days,

recycling

will create less waste.

And **you** can too.

Here's what to **do**...

Take something old,
make something **new!**

ONCE UPON A BIG...

Invention-wise, the wheel is our finest achievement. Apart from dung beetles rolling poo into balls, nothing else in nature has anything quite like it. Originally invented for use in pottery, wheels have allowed us to devise all our major forms of land transport. Other key inventions include language, the printing press, maps, medicine, electricity, the light bulb and the Internet.

Dangerous as it is, fire has been invaluable to humanity. With fire we could cook food, and it helped us to see and work at night. Fire eventually led to gunpowder and fuels, to foundries where we would work metals and to factories where we could manufacture a great many things from microscopes to mobiles, engines to electrical equipment.

Eco-kids are children who help with environmental issues at school. They have regular meetings to discuss how the school can be more eco-friendly. Do you have eco-kids at your school? If not, why don't you suggest the idea to your teacher? You could start by building your own bug or bee hotels from recyclables.

Animals are inventive creatures too; it's how they've learnt to survive. They've been doing clever stuff with natural resources for millennia. Sea otters use pebbles to break open shells. Birds build nests from twigs, grass, moss – even spider silk. Monkeys use sticks to help them catch termites. So, nature is naturally curious and creative!